TABLE OF CONTENTS

INTRODUCTION

Welcome to the world of QuickBooks Online; a powerful, intuitive, and indispensable tool designed to revolutionize the way you manage your finances. In today's fast-paced business landscape, staying on top of financial matters is not just crucial but a defining factor for success. And that's where QuickBooks Online steps in as your trusted ally.

QuickBooks Online is a cloud-based accounting software suite crafted to simplify and streamline financial management for businesses of all sizes. It provides a robust platform for organizing, tracking, and optimizing financial operations, all accessible at your fingertips from any internet-connected device.

Gone are the days of tedious manual data entry and complex spreadsheets; QuickBooks Online empowers users with a user-friendly interface, cutting-edge features, and seamless automation, allowing you to focus on what truly matters; growing your business.

Imagine having a tool that not only simplifies financial tasks but also offers real-time insights into your business's financial health. QuickBooks Online is more than just accounting software; it's a strategic partner that unlocks a multitude of benefits.

By harnessing the power of the cloud, QuickBooks Online grants you the freedom to access your financial data from anywhere with internet connectivity. Whether you're at the office, on the go, or working remotely, your financial insights are just a click away. With its user-friendly interface, QuickBooks Online makes organizing and categorizing financial data a breeze. From creating invoices to reconciling bank accounts, it offers a seamless experience for even the non-accountant.

Keep your financial records meticulously organized and accurate. From invoicing clients to tracking expenses and reconciling bank accounts, QuickBooks Online ensures precision in every transaction. Say goodbye to the hassle of manually tracking transactions, invoices, or expenses. QuickBooks Online automates these processes, providing real-time updates and ensuring accuracy in financial records.

Generate detailed financial reports effortlessly. Understand your business's financial performance, make informed decisions, and plan for the future with insightful reports and analytics. As your business grows, QuickBooks Online grows with you. Its scalability allows for easy integration with various third-party apps and additional features, adapting to the evolving needs of your enterprise.

QuickBooks Online isn't just about managing numbers; it's about empowering businesses to thrive. It's a tool that transcends traditional accounting, transforming financial management into a strategic advantage. Join the ranks of savvy businesses worldwide that have unlocked their full financial potential with QuickBooks Online.

Get ready to embark on a journey that simplifies financial complexities, saves precious time, and fuels the growth of your business. Welcome to QuickBooks Online; where financial management meets innovation.

CHAPTER ONE

WHAT IS QUICKBOOKS ONLINE?

QuickBooks Online is a cloud-based accounting software developed by Intuit, designed to help individuals, small businesses, and accountants manage their financial tasks efficiently. It's a powerful tool that offers a wide range of features and functionalities to streamline various aspects of accounting and financial management.

Key aspects of QuickBooks Online include:

• Cloud-Based Accessibility: QuickBooks Online operates entirely online, enabling users to access their financial data from any device with an internet connection. This accessibility allows for flexibility in managing finances from multiple locations or on-the-go.

• Core Financial Functions: The software covers essential accounting tasks such as invoicing, expense tracking, accounts receivable/payable management, bank reconciliation, and financial reporting. These features help businesses stay organized and maintain accurate financial records.

• User-Friendly Interface: QuickBooks Online provides an intuitive and user-friendly interface, making it accessible to individuals with varying levels of accounting knowledge. It's easy navigation and layout contribute to a smoother user experience.

• Customization and Scalability: The platform offers customizable features to suit different business needs. It's scalable, allowing businesses to adapt as they grow by offering different subscription plans and add-on services to accommodate expanding requirements.

• Integration and Third-Party Apps: QuickBooks Online integrates with a variety of third-party applications and services, allowing users to expand its functionality by connecting with tools for payroll, inventory management, e-commerce, CRM, and more.

• Automatic Updates and Security: Intuit regularly updates QuickBooks Online to add new features and enhance security measures. The software employs robust security protocols to protect sensitive financial data.

• Collaboration and Multiple Users: Users can collaborate with team members or accountants by granting access to specific features or data within QuickBooks Online, facilitating teamwork and efficient financial management.

Overall, QuickBooks Online simplifies accounting processes, saves time, and provides valuable insights into a business's financial health. It caters to a wide range of users, from sole proprietors and freelancers to small and medium-sized businesses, offering them a comprehensive solution to manage their finances effectively.

FEATURES OF QUICKBOOKS ONLINE

QuickBooks Online offers a diverse set of features designed to streamline accounting processes and aid in efficient financial management. Here's an overview of some key features available in QuickBooks Online:

Dashboard:

• Provides an overview of a business's financial health, including income, expenses, account balances, and recent activities.

• Quick access to important tasks, reminders, and reports.

Invoicing:

• Create and customize professional-looking invoices with company logos, payment terms, and item details.

• Send invoices directly to customers and track their payment status.

Expense Tracking:

• Record and categorize expenses, bills, and receipts by attaching images for documentation.

• Monitor spending and manage vendor payments efficiently.

Bank Reconciliation:

• Automatically import bank transactions and reconcile accounts to ensure accuracy.

• Match transactions, categorize them, and identify discrepancies easily.

Financial Reporting:

• Generate various financial reports such as balance sheets, profit and loss statements, cash flow statements, and customizable reports.

• Analyze business performance, monitor trends, and make informed decisions based on real-time data.

Accounts Receivable and Payable:

• Manage accounts receivable by tracking invoices and customer payments.

• Handle accounts payable by managing bills and vendor payments, ensuring timely settlements.

Inventory Management:

• Track inventory levels, sales, and purchase orders.

• Manage inventory items and stock quantities in real-time.

Payroll Processing:

• Run payroll, calculate taxes, and generate pay stubs for employees.

• Automate payroll tasks, including direct deposits and tax filings.

Time Tracking:

• Track billable hours by project or client for accurate invoicing.

• Monitor employee productivity and project profitability.

Integration with Third-Party Apps:

• Connect with various third-party applications and services, such as payment processors, CRM tools, e-commerce platforms, and more.

• Enhance functionality by integrating with specialized software to meet specific business needs.

Customization and Scalability:

• Customize invoices, reports, and templates to reflect brand identity.

• Scale with different subscription plans and add-on features as business requirements evolve.

Collaboration and User Access:

• Invite multiple users and set access levels to control what each user can view or modify.

• Facilitate collaboration between team members or accountants for seamless financial management.

These features collectively offer a comprehensive solution for businesses to efficiently manage their finances, streamline operations, and gain valuable insights into their financial performance using QuickBooks Online.

QuickBooks Online provides numerous advantages for businesses and individuals seeking streamlined financial management. Some of the key advantages include:

Accessibility and Convenience:

• Cloud-based platform accessible from any device with an internet connection, enabling users to manage finances from anywhere, anytime.

• No need for software installations or updates, allowing easy access to the latest features and data.

Ease of Use and User-Friendly Interface:

• Intuitive interface designed for users with varying levels of accounting expertise.

• Simple navigation and user-friendly design make it accessible for beginners while offering robust tools for experienced users.

Time and Efficiency Savings:

• Automation of repetitive tasks such as invoicing, expense tracking, and bank reconciliation saves time and reduces manual data entry errors.

• Streamlined workflows and features like automatic syncing with bank accounts expedite financial processes.

Accurate Financial Tracking and Reporting:

• Enables accurate tracking of income, expenses, invoices, and payments, leading to better financial control and decision-making.

• Generates comprehensive reports (profit and loss, balance sheets, cash flow statements, etc.) offering insights into business performance.

Customization and Scalability:

• Allows customization of invoices, templates, and reports to reflect the brand identity and specific business needs.

• Scalable platform offering different subscription plans and add-ons to accommodate business growth and evolving requirements.

Collaboration and Accessibility for Multiple Users:

• Multiple users can collaborate simultaneously, with customized access levels for different team members or accountants.

• Facilitates teamwork by allowing real-time collaboration and data sharing among authorized users.

Security and Reliability:

• Utilizes robust security measures and encryption protocols to protect sensitive financial data.

• Regular updates and backups ensure data security and reliability.

Integration with Third-Party Apps:

• Seamlessly integrates with a wide range of third-party applications and services, enhancing functionality and extending capabilities to suit specific business needs.

- Connects with payment processors, CRM tools, e-commerce platforms, and more for a comprehensive business solution.

Customer Support and Resources:

- Access to customer support, tutorials, guides, and online resources offered by Intuit for troubleshooting and learning purposes.

- Community forums and expert advice available for additional assistance and insights.

Overall, QuickBooks Online offers a versatile and efficient accounting solution that empowers businesses to manage their finances effectively, improve productivity, and make informed decisions based on accurate financial data.

QUICKBOOKS ONLINE VERSIONS AVAILABLE

QuickBooks Online offers several versions or subscription plans tailored to different business needs and sizes. Here are some of the main versions available:

Simple Start:

• Ideal for freelancers, self-employed individuals, and small businesses.

• Basic features include income and expense tracking, invoicing, and basic reporting.

Essentials:

• Suitable for small to medium-sized businesses with additional needs.

• Includes features from Simple Start with added capabilities like managing bills, multiple users, and more robust reporting.

Plus:

• Designed for growing businesses that require advanced functionalities.

• Includes all features from Essentials with added inventory tracking, project profitability tracking, and time tracking.

- Tailored for larger businesses with complex needs.

- Offers advanced reporting, batch invoicing, customizable access by role, dedicated account management, and enhanced support.

These versions differ in their feature sets, scalability, and pricing structures. They cater to businesses of varying sizes, from sole proprietors and startups to larger enterprises, offering a range of capabilities to meet different accounting and financial management requirements.

Pricing Structure:

The pricing for QuickBooks Online plans may vary based on promotions, features included, and the number of users. Typically, QuickBooks Online operates on a subscription-based model with monthly or annual payment options.

Additional factors that might affect pricing:

- Promotional offers or discounts for new subscribers.

• The number of users accessing the account.

• Additional services or add-ons chosen (e.g., payroll, payment processing).

Considerations:

• QuickBooks often offers discounts or promotions, especially for new users or during certain periods.

• Pricing may vary by region or country due to local taxes and currency differences.

• QuickBooks occasionally updates its plans and features, so it's recommended to check their official website for the most up-to-date information.

For the latest pricing details, including any changes in plans, features, or promotional offers, it's best to visit the QuickBooks website or contact their sales/customer service directly.

SYSTEM REqUIREMENTS AND COMPATIBILITY OF QUICKBOOKS ONLINE

QuickBooks Online is a cloud-based accounting software, and as such, it primarily operates through a web browser. Hence, it doesn't have traditional system requirements like locally installed software. However, users need to ensure their devices meet certain basic requirements to access and use QuickBooks Online effectively:

Device Requirements:

• Internet Connection: A stable and reasonably fast internet connection is essential for accessing QuickBooks Online. High-speed internet improves performance.

• Supported Browsers: QuickBooks Online is compatible with most modern web browsers such as Google Chrome, Mozilla Firefox, Microsoft Edge, Safari, etc. It's recommended to use the latest versions for optimal performance.

• Compatibility: QuickBooks Online is compatible with various devices and operating systems:

• Operating Systems: Windows, macOS, Linux and Chrome OS

• Devices: Desktops (Windows and Mac), Laptops, Tablets (iPad, Android tablets) and Smartphones (iOS and Android)

Additional Considerations:

• For optimal experience and functionality, it's recommended to use the latest version of a supported browser.

• Ensure that cookies, JavaScript, and pop-ups are enabled in the browser settings for QuickBooks Online to function correctly.

• QuickBooks Online mobile apps are available for iOS and Android devices, offering limited functionality compared to the web version but providing convenient access on the go.

While QuickBooks Online doesn't have stringent system requirements in the traditional sense, users should prioritize having a stable internet connection and using a compatible, up-to-date web browser for the best user experience and performance.

THE SIGNIFICANCE OF QUICKBOOKS ONLINE FOR MANAGING FINANCES

QuickBooks Online holds significant importance in managing finances for businesses of various sizes and individuals due to several reasons:

• Automation and Efficiency: QuickBooks Online automates various financial tasks, including invoicing, expense tracking, and bank reconciliations. This automation saves time and reduces the potential for human error, enabling businesses to focus on core operations.

• Accessibility and Mobility: Being a cloud-based solution, QuickBooks Online allows users to access financial data from anywhere with an internet connection. This accessibility offers flexibility for business owners, accountants, and employees to manage finances on-the-go or from multiple locations.

• Real-Time Insights: The software provides real-time access to financial information. Users can generate reports instantly, allowing for better decision-making based on up-to-date data. This timely insight into the financial health of the business aids in strategic planning and forecasting.

• Accuracy and Organization: QuickBooks Online helps maintain accurate and organized financial records. From tracking income and expenses to managing accounts payable and receivable, the platform ensures meticulous recording and categorization of financial data.

• Customization and Scalability: It offers customizable features and is scalable to accommodate different business needs. Users can customize invoices, reports, and templates to align with their branding and business requirements. Additionally, the software adapts as businesses grow or change in size and complexity.

• Financial Control and Compliance: QuickBooks Online facilitates better financial control by allowing businesses to monitor cash flow, track budgets, and manage taxes efficiently. It also helps in meeting compliance requirements by accurately recording and reporting financial transactions.

• Integration with Third-Party Apps: It integrates with various third-party applications and services, expanding its functionality. Users can connect with payment processors, CRM tools, inventory management systems, and other software, enhancing overall business operations.

• Collaboration and Multi-User Access: QuickBooks Online allows multiple users with different access levels, enabling collaboration among team members or accountants. This feature promotes teamwork and efficient sharing of financial data while controlling user permissions.

• Support and Updates: QuickBooks Online provides customer support, tutorials, and resources to help users navigate the software effectively. Regular updates and improvements ensure the software stays up-to-date with the latest features and security measures.

In summary, QuickBooks Online plays a crucial role in simplifying financial management, improving accuracy, offering real-time insights, and providing the tools necessary for businesses to make informed decisions, ultimately contributing to their financial success and growth.

CHAPTER TWO

QUICKBOOKS ONLINE SPECIFIC TERMINOLOGIES

QuickBooks Online has specific terminologies related to its features and functionalities. Here are some key terminologies commonly used within QuickBooks Online:

1. Chart of Accounts Terminology:

• Accounts: Represents categories where financial transactions are recorded (e.g., bank accounts, assets, liabilities, income, expenses).

• Account Types: Classifies accounts into categories like Bank, Expense, Income, Liability, Asset, Equity, and Cost of Goods Sold.

2. Transactions:

• Invoices: Documents sent to customers detailing products or services sold, including payment terms.

• Bills: Records of amounts owed to vendors for products or services received.

• Payments: Records of money paid by customers against invoices or money paid to vendors against bills.

• Expenses: Records of business-related expenses incurred, categorized by type (e.g., office supplies, utilities).

3. Banking:

• Bank Feeds: Automatic updates of bank and credit card transactions into QuickBooks Online.

• Reconciliation: Matching transactions in QuickBooks Online with bank statements to ensure accuracy.

4. Reports:

• Profit and Loss (P&L): Summarizes revenues, expenses, and net profit over a specific period.

• Balance Sheet: Displays a company's financial position, showing assets, liabilities, and equity at a specific point in time.

• Cash Flow Statement: Shows cash inflows and outflows from operating, investing, and financing activities.

5. Customers and Sales:

• Customers: Individuals or entities who purchase products or services from your business.

• Sales Receipts: Records of sales transactions completed at the point of sale.

• Estimates: Quotations or proposals given to customers detailing anticipated costs for products or services.

6. Vendors and Purchases:

• Vendors: Individuals or entities from whom your business purchases goods or services.

• Purchase Orders: Documents requesting goods or services from vendors before a transaction occurs.

• Credit Memos: Records issued to customers for returned goods or services, crediting their accounts.

7. Customization:

• Custom Form Styles: Allows customization of invoices, estimates, and other forms with personalized layouts and branding.

• Custom Fields: Additional fields that can be added to records to capture specific information beyond standard fields.

8. Payroll:

• Payroll: Management of employee salaries, taxes, and benefits.

• Payroll Liabilities: Amounts owed by the company for payroll taxes, employee benefits, and other payroll-related expenses.

9. Accountant-Specific Features:

• Accountant Tools: Specialized functionalities available to accountants or bookkeepers to manage multiple clients or perform specific accounting tasks efficiently.

• Journal Entries: Manual entries used by accountants to record adjustments or corrections directly into specific accounts.

10. Apps and Integrations:

• QuickBooks Apps: Third-party applications that integrate with QuickBooks Online to extend functionality or provide specialized features (e.g., CRM, inventory management, time tracking).

Understanding these specific terminologies within QuickBooks Online will facilitate better navigation and utilization of its features, aiding in effective financial management for your business.

HOW TO USE THE QUICKBOOKS ONLINE SOFTWARE

Using QuickBooks Online involves several steps to set up, navigate, and perform various accounting tasks. Here's a general guide on how to use QuickBooks Online:

1. Account Setup:

• Create an Account: Sign up for QuickBooks Online and select the appropriate subscription plan for your business needs.

• Company Profile Setup: Enter your business details, such as company name, industry, address, and fiscal year start.

2. Navigation:

• Dashboard Overview: Upon login, you'll see the dashboard displaying an overview of your business finances, including income, expenses, bank accounts, and more.

• Navigation Menu: Use the left-hand navigation menu to access different modules like Sales, Expenses, Banking, Reports, Taxes, and more.

3. Data Entry:

• Transactions: Enter transactions like invoices, expenses, bills, and payments using the "+" sign or respective tabs in the navigation menu.

• Banking: Connect bank and credit card accounts to QuickBooks Online for automatic transaction imports or manually upload bank statements.

4. Reports and Analysis:

• Generate Reports: Explore and create various financial reports such as profit and loss, balance sheet, cash flow, and custom reports for detailed insights.

• Analysis: Use reports to analyze business performance, monitor trends, and make informed financial decisions.

5. Customization:

• Customization Options: Customize invoices, estimates, and other forms with your logo, preferred layout, and fields using the "Custom Form Styles" option.

• Chart of Accounts: Customize your chart of accounts to organize finances based on your business structure and needs.

6. Integration and Add-ons:

• Integrate Apps: Explore the QuickBooks App Store to integrate third-party apps that extend functionality or streamline specific processes.

• Add-ons: Consider specialized add-ons for industry-specific needs or enhanced features beyond the core QuickBooks Online capabilities.

7. Help and Support:

• Help Center: Access the QuickBooks Online Help Center or use in-platform resources for tutorials, guides, and FAQs.

• Customer Support: Contact QuickBooks Online customer support for assistance with technical issues or queries.

Notes:

• QuickBooks Online offers multiple tutorials, webinars, and help resources to guide users through various tasks and features.

• Consider exploring sample company files provided by QuickBooks Online to practice using the software in a demo environment.

STEP-BY-STEP GUIDE ON CREATING A QUICKBOOKS ONLINE ACCOUNT

Creating a QuickBooks Online account involves a few straightforward steps. Here's a step-by-step guide to help you get started:

Step 1: Access QuickBooks Online Website

• Open a web browser and navigate to the official QuickBooks Online website.

Step 2: Sign Up for a New Account

• On the QuickBooks Online website, locate and click on the "Sign Up" or "Try it free" button.

• You'll be directed to the sign-up page. Choose the version of QuickBooks Online that suits your needs (Simple Start, Essentials, Plus, or Advanced).

• Enter your email address and create a secure password for your QuickBooks Online account.

• Click on "Try it free" or "Sign Up" to start the registration process.

Step 3: Provide Business Information

• Fill in the required business information, including your business name, type of business, industry, and contact details.

• Follow the prompts to provide additional information such as your business address, phone number, and tax identification number (if applicable).

Step 4: Customize Your Account

• Customize your QuickBooks Online account settings. This includes selecting your currency, fiscal year start date, and other preferences according to your business needs.

Step 5: Choose Add-Ons (If Needed)

• Optionally, you may choose to add extra services or features such as payroll or payment processing during the registration process.

Step 6: Explore the Dashboard

• Once your account is set up, you'll be directed to the QuickBooks Online dashboard. Take some time to explore the dashboard, which includes various features and navigation options.

Step 7: Add Financial Information

• Start entering your financial information, such as bank accounts, income, expenses, customers, vendors, and any existing financial data. You can manually input this information or import data from other sources.

Step 8: Familiarize Yourself with Features

• Familiarize yourself with the features available in QuickBooks Online by exploring different tabs and sections within the software. This includes invoicing, expense tracking, reporting, and more.

Step 9: Learn and Utilize Resources

• Take advantage of QuickBooks Online's tutorials, help articles, videos, and customer support resources to learn more about using the platform effectively.

Step 10: Start Using QuickBooks Online

• Start using QuickBooks Online for your daily financial management tasks. Create invoices, track expenses, reconcile accounts, and generate reports to manage your business efficiently.

By following these steps, you can create a QuickBooks Online account and begin using the platform to streamline your business's financial processes.

STEP-BY-STEP GUIDE TO SETTING UP A COMPANY PROFILE ON QUICKBOOKS ONLINE

Setting up a company profile in QuickBooks Online involves several essential steps to ensure accurate and organized financial management. Here's a detailed step-by-step guide:

Step 1: Access QuickBooks Online Dashboard

• Log in to your QuickBooks Online account using your credentials.

Step 2: Access Company Settings

• From the QuickBooks Online dashboard, navigate to the gear icon (⚙) at the top right corner and select "Account and Settings" under Your Company.

Step 3: Set Up Company Profile Information

• In the Account and Settings section, click on the "Company" tab or a similar option (may vary depending on the QuickBooks version).

Review and update essential company information such as:

• Company name, address, and contact details.

• Legal entity type (sole proprietorship, LLC, corporation, etc.).

• Business type or industry.

• Business ID or Tax ID.

Step 4: Customize Company Preferences

Explore and adjust company preferences in the Account and Settings section based on your business needs. This may include setting up preferences for:

• Time zone, date format, and fiscal year start.

• Currency used for transactions.

• Default email messages for customer communications (like invoices or estimates).

Step 5: Add Additional Company Details (Optional)

Under the Company tab or a related section, input additional information as needed:

• Business description or mission statement.

• Logo and branding (if desired) to customize invoices and reports.

• Social media handles or website information.

Step 6: Set Up Tax Settings

• Navigate to the "Sales Tax" or "Taxes" section within Account and Settings.

• Set up sales tax settings if applicable to your business, including tax agency details, tax rates, and collection preferences.

Step 7: Save Changes

• After making all necessary adjustments and configurations, ensure to click "Save" or "Done" at the bottom of the page to apply the changes to your company profile settings.

Step 8: Review and Update Periodically

• Periodically revisit your company settings to ensure all information remains accurate and up-to-date, especially if there are changes in business details, tax regulations, or preferences.

Step 9: Explore Additional Features

• Take time to explore other areas of QuickBooks Online related to company settings, such as sales, expenses, payments, and reports, to further customize and optimize your financial management.

By following these steps, you can set up a comprehensive company profile in QuickBooks Online, ensuring that your financial records and settings accurately reflect your business details and preferences.

STEP-BY-STEP GUIDE ON ADDING USERS ON QUICKBOOKS ONLINE

Adding users to QuickBooks Online involves a few steps to grant access to your company's financial data. Here's a step-by-step guide:

Step 1: Access User Settings

• Log in to your QuickBooks Online account as the Admin or Master Admin.

• From the QuickBooks Online dashboard, click the gear icon (⚙) in the top right corner.

• Select "Manage Users" or "Users and Permissions" under Your Company.

Step 2: Add New User

• In the User Management section, click the "Add user" or "Invite" button.

Step 3: Enter User Details

Fill in the new user's details:

• Email address: Enter the email of the person you want to invite.

• First name and Last name: Provide the user's name.

• User type: Choose the appropriate user access level (Regular or Custom user, or Admin).

Step 4: Assign Access Rights

Define the user's access rights and permissions:

• For a Regular User: Assign specific roles (such as sales, reports, expenses) or limit access based on predefined roles.

• For a Custom User: Customize access by selecting specific areas or features they can view or modify.

Step 5: Review and Send Invitation

• Review the user's details and access permissions to ensure accuracy.

• Once confirmed, click "Save" or "Invite" to send the invitation to the new user.

Step 6: New User Accepts Invitation

• The invited user receives an email invitation from QuickBooks Online.

• The user should open the email and follow the instructions to accept the invitation to join the company's QuickBooks Online account.

Step 7: Set Up Account

• If the user is new to QuickBooks Online, they will need to set up their account by creating a password and completing their profile.

Step 8: User Accesses QuickBooks Online

• After completing the setup, the user can log in to QuickBooks Online using their credentials.

Step 9: Manage Users (Admin's Perspective)

• As an Admin, revisit the Manage Users section to make changes to user access, permissions, or to delete users if necessary.

Notes:

• Each subscription plan in QuickBooks Online has a limit on the number of users allowed.

• The Admin or Master Admin has complete control over user access and permissions.

• Regular users have access as per the permissions granted by the Admin.

• Regularly review and update user access to maintain data security and integrity.

By following these steps, you can successfully add new users to your QuickBooks Online account and manage their access rights and permissions based on your company's needs.

HOW TO MANAGE PERMISSIONS ON QUICKBOOKS ONLINE

Managing permissions in QuickBooks Online involves controlling what users can access and modify within the company's financial data. Here's a step-by-step guide on how to manage permissions:

Step 1: Access User Management

• Log in to your QuickBooks Online account as the Admin or Master Admin.

• From the QuickBooks Online dashboard, click the gear icon (⚙) in the top right corner.

• Select "Manage Users" or "Users and Permissions" under Your Company.

Step 2: Review Existing Users and Permissions

• In the User Management section, you'll see a list of current users along with their access levels and roles.

• Identify the user for whom you want to modify permissions or review the current settings.

Step 3: Edit User Permissions

• Locate the user you want to manage and click on their name or the "Edit" or "Edit user" option next to their name.

Step 4: Modify User Access

In the Edit User window or Permissions section:

For a Regular User:

• Assign predefined roles or permissions (such as Sales, Reports, Expenses) by ticking the corresponding checkboxes.

• Use the predefined roles or customize permissions by allowing or restricting access to specific areas or features within QuickBooks Online.

For a Custom User:

• Customize access by selecting or deselecting specific areas, functions, or modules based on your preferences.

• Check or uncheck the boxes to grant or restrict access to various features, transactions, and reports.

Step 5: Save Changes

• After adjusting the user's permissions, review the changes made.

• Click "Save" or "Save and Close" to apply the modified permissions to the user's account.

Step 6: Verify Changes

• Ensure that the changes to user permissions are correctly applied by reviewing the user's access levels and limitations.

Step 7: Repeat for Other Users (If Needed)

• Repeat the process for other users if you need to modify their permissions or access levels.

Notes:

• The Admin or Master Admin has the authority to manage and adjust user permissions within QuickBooks Online.

• Regularly review and update user access to maintain data security and compliance.

• QuickBooks Online offers predefined roles and custom permission settings to suit various business needs.

By following these steps, you can effectively manage and customize user permissions in QuickBooks Online, allowing you to control access to sensitive financial data and ensure that users have appropriate access levels based on their roles within the organization.

HOW TO NAVIGATE QUICKBOOKS ONLINE USER INTERFACE

Navigating the QuickBooks Online user interface is crucial for effectively managing your financial data and utilizing its features. Here's a step-by-step guide to help you navigate through the QuickBooks Online interface:

Step 1: Log In to QuickBooks Online

• Open your web browser and log in to your QuickBooks Online account using your credentials (username and password).

Step 2: Explore the Dashboard

• Once logged in, you'll land on the QuickBooks Online dashboard.

• The dashboard provides an overview of your business's financial health, including income, expenses, account balances, and other important insights.

Step 3: Navigate the Left-side Menu

Explore the left-side menu, which is the primary navigation area:

• Dashboard: Provides an overview of your company's financial status.

• Sales: Access customer-related transactions such as invoices, sales receipts, and customers' lists.

• Expenses: Manage and track business expenses, bills, and vendors.

• Banking: Connect and manage bank accounts, review transactions, and reconcile accounts.

• Reports: Generate various financial reports like profit and loss, balance sheet, and more.

• Taxes: Access tax-related features, such as sales tax and tax-related reports.

• Accounting: Manage charts of accounts, reconciliation, and other accounting tasks.

• Apps: Access third-party apps that integrate with QuickBooks Online.

• Other Features: Depending on your subscription plan, you might have additional features or tabs.

Step 4: Use the Top Navigation Bar

Explore the top navigation bar for additional functionalities:

• Create (+): Access options to create new transactions like invoices, expenses, and more.

• Search (magnifying glass icon): Quickly search for transactions, customers, or reports.

• Quick Create (plus icon): Shortcut to create new transactions directly from the dashboard.

• Help (?): Access help, tutorials, and support options.

• Settings (gear icon): Manage company settings, account and settings, and user permissions.

Step 5: Customize and Personalize

Customize your QuickBooks Online interface:

• Click on the gear icon (⚙) to access "Account and Settings" to personalize your company settings.

• Customize reports, templates, and preferences according to your business needs.

Step 6: Access Additional Features

• Depending on your subscription plan, explore additional features available in QuickBooks Online such as payroll, inventory, time tracking, and more. These features may have their sections or tabs in the left-side menu.

Step 7: Log Out Securely

• After completing your tasks, log out of your QuickBooks Online account for security purposes.

Notes:

• Familiarize yourself with various sections, tabs, and functionalities within QuickBooks Online to efficiently manage your financial data.

• QuickBooks Online's interface may slightly vary based on the version or updates released after this guide's creation.

• Utilize help resources, tutorials, and customer support if you encounter any issues or need guidance while navigating QuickBooks Online.

By following these steps, you can effectively navigate the QuickBooks Online user interface and access its various features and functionalities to manage your business's financial data.

STEP-BY-STEP INSTRUCTIONS ON CUSTOMIZING PREFERENCES

Customizing preferences in QuickBooks Online allows you to tailor the software to match your business's specific needs and workflows. Here's a step-by-step guide on how to customize preferences:

Step-by-Step Guide to Customizing Preferences in QuickBooks Online:

Access Account and Settings:

• Log in to your QuickBooks Online account as an Admin or Master Admin.

• Click the gear icon (⚙) in the top right corner.

Select "Account and Settings":

• From the drop-down menu, select "Account and Settings" or "Company Settings" under Your Company.

Navigate Preferences:

• In the Account and Settings menu, you'll find several tabs on the left side, such as Company, Billing & Subscription, Sales, Expenses, Payments, Advanced, etc.

• Click on each tab to review and customize preferences according to your business requirements.

Customize Preferences:

Review and modify settings in each tab based on your business needs:

• Company Settings: Adjust settings related to company details, company type, fiscal year, and communication preferences.

• Billing & Subscription (if applicable): Manage subscription and billing-related preferences.

• Sales: Customize settings related to sales forms (invoices, estimates), sales form content, and messages.

• Expenses: Modify preferences for expense-related settings, such as bills and expenses, purchase orders, and items and categories.

• Payments: Adjust settings for payment-related preferences, such as payment processing, payment reminders, and online payments.

• Advanced: Explore advanced settings including automation, time tracking, and other advanced preferences.

Save Changes:

• After making adjustments in each tab, ensure to click "Save" or "Save and Done" at the bottom of the tab to apply the changes.

Review Customizations:

• Double-check your changes to ensure they align with your business requirements.

Exit Account and Settings:

• Click on the "X" or "Close" button to exit the Account and Settings menu and return to the main QuickBooks Online interface.

Notes:

• Take your time to review each preference setting and make adjustments that best fit your business's needs.

• Be cautious while making changes to avoid unintended modifications that may affect your financial records.

• Preferences can significantly impact how QuickBooks Online operates for your business, so ensure you understand the implications of the changes made.

By following these steps, you can efficiently customize preferences in QuickBooks Online to match your business requirements and optimize the software for streamlined financial management.

STEP-BY-STEP INSTRUCTIONS ON CUSTOMIZING TEMPLATES

Customizing templates in QuickBooks Online allows you to personalize the look and feel of your invoices, estimates, sales receipts, and other forms to match your brand and business needs. Here's a step-by-step guide on how to customize templates:

Step-by-Step Guide to Customizing Templates in QuickBooks Online:

Access Custom Form Styles:

• Log in to your QuickBooks Online account as an Admin or Master Admin.

• Click the gear icon (⚙) in the top right corner.

Select "Custom Form Styles":

• From the drop-down menu, select "Custom Form Styles" under Your Company.

Choose New Style or Edit an Existing Style:

• Click the "New style" button to create a new template or select an existing template to edit.

Select Form Type:

• Choose the type of form you want to customize (e.g., Invoice, Estimate, Sales Receipt, etc.).

Customize the Template:

Once in the customization window, you'll find options to modify the layout, design, and content of the form:

• Design Tab: Customize the appearance of the form by changing colors, fonts, logos, and adding a custom header or footer.

• Content Tab: Modify the content of the form, such as adding or removing fields, rearranging sections, and changing the column layout. Click on a section to edit or customize it.

• Email Tab (if available): Adjust settings related to email delivery, such as email subject, message, and attachment options for the form.

• Print Tab (if available): Customize how the form appears when printed, including paper size, margins, and print settings.

Preview Changes:

• Use the preview option to see how the customized template will look.

Save Customizations:

• After making changes, click "Done" or "Save" to save your customized template.

Apply the Customized Template:

• Once saved, the customized template will be available to use when creating invoices, estimates, or other forms.

Notes:

• Take your time to design and customize the template to align with your brand identity.

• Ensure the layout and content are easy to understand for your customers and contain all necessary information.

• Preview the template to ensure it meets your expectations before saving the changes.

By following these steps, you can efficiently customize templates in QuickBooks Online to create professional-looking forms that match your brand and meet your business requirements.

STEP-BY-STEP INSTRUCTIONS ON CUSTOMIZING CHART OF ACCOUNTS

Customizing the Chart of Accounts in QuickBooks Online allows you to tailor your account categories to better suit your business needs. Here's a step-by-step guide on how to customize the Chart of Accounts:

Step-by-Step Guide to Customizing Chart of Accounts in QuickBooks Online:

Access Chart of Accounts:

• Log in to your QuickBooks Online account as an Admin or Master Admin.

• From the left-side menu, select "Accounting" and then click on "Chart of Accounts."

View Existing Accounts:

• Review the existing accounts listed in the Chart of Accounts.

Edit an Existing Account:

• To modify an account, find the account you want to edit and click on the drop-down arrow under the "Action" column.

• Select "Edit" to modify the account details.

Edit Account Details:

• In the Edit Account window, modify the account details such as Account Name, Account Type, Detail Type, Description, and other relevant information.

• Make necessary changes to suit your business needs.

Add a New Account:

• To add a new account, click the "New" button.

• Select the Account Type (e.g., Bank, Expense, Income, Liability, etc.) for the new account.

• Fill in the necessary details such as Account Name, Detail Type, Description, and other relevant information.

• Save the new account.

Delete an Account (if necessary):

• To delete an account, locate the account you want to delete.

• Click on the drop-down arrow under the "Action" column.

• Select "Delete."

Note: You can only delete accounts that don't have associated transactions. If transactions are linked to the account, you may have to make them inactive instead of deleting them.

Reorder Accounts (if needed):

• To change the order of accounts, click and drag an account to the desired position within the Chart of Accounts.

• This can help organize accounts in a more logical or preferred sequence.

Save Changes:

• After making modifications or adding new accounts, ensure to click "Save" to update the Chart of Accounts.

Notes:

• Be cautious while editing or deleting accounts, especially those with transactions linked to them, as it can impact your financial records.

• Customize the Chart of Accounts to better categorize and organize your financial transactions for easier reporting and analysis.

• Consider using subaccounts or parent-child relationships within the Chart of Accounts to further organize and group related accounts.

By following these steps, you can efficiently customize the Chart of Accounts in QuickBooks Online to better reflect your business's financial structure and reporting needs.

STEP-BY-STEP INSTRUCTIONS ON CUSTOMIZING REPORTS

Customizing reports in QuickBooks Online allows you to tailor the reports to meet your specific business needs, providing insights and data relevant to your operations. Here's a step-by-step guide on how to customize reports:

Step-by-Step Guide to Customizing Reports in QuickBooks Online:

Access Reports:

• Log in to your QuickBooks Online account as an Admin or Master Admin.

• Click on the "Reports" tab from the left-side menu.

Select a Report:

• Choose the report you want to customize from the list of available reports.

• Click on the report name to generate it.

Adjust Report Settings:

Once the report is open, you'll find customization options at the top of the report window:

• Date Range: Adjust the date range to view data for a specific period.

• Columns: Modify columns to include or exclude certain data columns in the report.

• Rows: Customize rows to add or remove certain rows or subtotals in the report.

• Filters: Apply filters to focus on specific criteria such as accounts, customers, products, etc.

• Group By: Group data in the report by specific criteria like date, customer, location, etc.

Customize Report Header/Footer (if available):

• Some reports allow customization of headers or footers with company information or additional notes.

• Look for customization options related to headers or footers within the report settings.

Save Customization (if available):

• If you want to save the customized report for future use with the same settings, check if there's an option to save customization.

• Give the report a name to save it for easy access.

Run the Customized Report:

• After making the necessary customizations, run the report to view the data based on your settings.

Export or Print (if needed):

• Utilize options to export the report to Excel, PDF, or print it for further analysis or sharing.

Save Customization Settings (if applicable):

• Some reports allow you to save customization settings for future use. If available, save the customization to access it later without reconfiguring.

Notes:

• Take your time to customize reports to display relevant data and insights tailored to your business needs.

• Experiment with different customization options to see which settings provide the most useful information.

• Ensure to review the report after customization to verify that it meets your requirements.

By following these steps, you can effectively customize reports in QuickBooks Online, allowing you to generate insights and data that are specifically relevant and beneficial for your business operations.

CHAPTER THREE

HOW TO CREATE INVOICES

Creating invoices in QuickBooks Online is a fundamental process for billing your customers for products or services rendered. Here's a step-by-step guide on how to create an invoice:

Step-by-Step Guide to Creating Invoices in QuickBooks Online:

Access the Invoices Section:

• Log in to your QuickBooks Online account as an Admin or user with invoicing permissions.

• From the left-side menu, select "Sales" or "Invoicing."

Click on "New Invoice":

• Look for the "New Invoice" button and click on it to create a new invoice.

Fill in Customer Details:

• Select the customer or client from the drop-down menu or add a new customer if necessary.

• Ensure the customer's billing information is correct and complete.

Choose Invoice Date and Due Date:

• Set the invoice date (the date the invoice is issued) and the due date (the date payment is expected).

Add Products/Services:

• In the "Product/Service" column, start typing the name of the item or service you're invoicing for.

• Choose the item from the drop-down list or add a new one if it's not already in your list of products/services.

• Enter the quantity, rate, and any applicable discounts or taxes.

Add Additional Details (if needed):

• Include a memo or notes for specific details related to the invoice.

• Attach any relevant documents or files if necessary.

Review and Save the Invoice:

• Double-check all details for accuracy, including customer information, item details, quantities, rates, and totals.

• Once reviewed, click "Save and Close" or "Save and New" to save the invoice.

Send the Invoice (optional):

• If you're ready to send the invoice immediately, click on "Save and send" to email the invoice to your customer directly from QuickBooks Online.

• Alternatively, you can save the invoice and send it later via email or print a hard copy to mail to your customer.

Track Invoice Status:

• Track the status of your invoices in the "Sales" or "Invoicing" section to see which ones are paid, pending, or overdue.

Notes:

• Customize invoice templates as per your business branding and preferences through the "Custom Form Styles" in the Account and Settings menu.

• QuickBooks Online automatically tracks the status of your invoices, helping you monitor payments and follow up on overdue invoices.

• Ensure to regularly reconcile payments received against your invoices to maintain accurate financial records.

By following these steps, you can efficiently create invoices in QuickBooks Online to bill your customers for products or services, helping streamline your billing process and keeping your financial records organized.

HOW TO MANAGE EXPENSES USING
QUICKBOOKS ONLINE

Managing expenses in QuickBooks Online involves tracking and categorizing your business expenditures. Here's a step-by-step guide on how to manage expenses:

Step-by-Step Guide to Managing Expenses in QuickBooks Online:

Access the Expenses Section:

• Log in to your QuickBooks Online account as an Admin or user with expenses permissions.

• From the left-side menu, select "Expenses" or "Transactions" and choose "Expenses."

Record New Expense:

• Click on the "New Transaction" or "New Expense" button.

Select Expense Category:

• Choose the appropriate expense category or account for the expense from the drop-down menu.

• Specify the payment account used for the expense (e.g., bank account, credit card).

Enter Expense Details:

• Fill in the expense details including the date, payee (vendor or supplier), amount, and description.

• Optionally, attach receipts or documents related to the expense.

Categorize Expenses:

• Assign the expense to the relevant category or create a new category if needed (e.g., office supplies, utilities, travel, etc.).

• This categorization helps in tracking and analyzing expenses for reporting purposes.

Add Sales Tax (if applicable):

• If the expense includes sales tax, specify the tax amount and choose the appropriate tax agency.

Save the Expense:

• Review all details for accuracy, then click "Save and close" or "Save and new" to save the expense entry.

Recurring Expenses (if applicable):

• For recurring expenses (such as monthly subscriptions or utilities), set up recurring transactions to automate entries.

Bank Feeds Integration (optional):

• Use the Bank Feeds feature to connect your bank accounts and credit cards, allowing for easier expense tracking and reconciliation.

• Match expenses entered manually with bank transactions for accuracy.

Expense Reports and Analysis:

• Utilize QuickBooks Online's reporting features to generate expense reports for a specific period, vendor, or category.

• Analyze spending patterns and review expense reports to gain insights into your business expenditures.

Notes:

• Regularly review and categorize expenses to maintain accurate financial records and better understand your business's spending patterns.

• Take advantage of QuickBooks Online's features like Bank Feeds and reporting tools to streamline expense tracking and analysis.

• Customize expense categories and preferences in Account and Settings to align with your business's needs.

By following these steps, you can effectively manage expenses in QuickBooks Online, allowing you to track, categorize, and analyze your business expenditures for better financial management.

HOW TO RECORD PAYMENTS USING QUICKBOOKS ONLINE

Recording payments in QuickBooks Online involves registering the money received against invoices or sales. Here's a step-by-step guide on how to record payments:

Step-by-Step Guide to Recording Payments in QuickBooks Online:

Access the Sales or Invoices Section:

• Log in to your QuickBooks Online account as an Admin or user with payment permissions.

• From the left-side menu, select "Sales" or "Invoicing."

View Open Invoices:

• Click on the "Invoices" or "Customers" tab to view a list of open invoices awaiting payment.

Select an Invoice for Payment:

• Choose the invoice for which you want to record a payment by clicking on it.

Record Payment:

• Within the invoice view, locate the "Receive payment" button or a similar option.

• Click on "Receive payment" to register the payment for that specific invoice.

Enter Payment Details:

Fill in the payment details:

• Payment Date: Specify the date the payment was received.

• Payment Method: Choose the method of payment (e.g., cash, check, credit card).

• Amount Received: Enter the amount received from the customer.

• Account Deposited To: Select the bank or account where the payment will be deposited.

• Reference Number (optional): Add a reference number or check number if applicable.

Apply Payment to the Invoice:

• In the "Outstanding Transactions" section, ensure the correct invoice is selected for payment application.

• The payment amount should match or be less than the invoice amount.

• If the payment is for multiple invoices, you can split the payment accordingly.

Save the Payment:

• Review all payment details for accuracy.

• Click "Save and close" or "Save and new" to record the payment and return to the invoice list.

Verify the Updated Invoice Status:

• Check the status of the invoice to ensure it's marked as "Paid" or "Closed."

Notes:

• QuickBooks Online automatically updates your accounts and financial statements when payments are recorded against invoices.

• Use the "Receive Payment" feature for cash, checks, or other received payments and apply them accurately to the respective invoices.

• Regularly reconcile payments to ensure they match your bank deposits for accurate bookkeeping.

By following these steps, you can effectively record payments in QuickBooks Online, accurately documenting money received against specific invoices or sales for proper financial tracking and reporting.

HOW TO CREATE ESTIMATES

Creating estimates in QuickBooks Online helps in providing potential customers with quotes for products or services before a sale. Here's a step-by-step guide on how to create estimates:

Step-by-Step Guide to Creating Estimates in QuickBooks Online:

Access the Estimates Section:

• Log in to your QuickBooks Online account as an Admin or user with estimate permissions.

• From the left-side menu, select "Sales" or "Invoicing."

Navigate to Estimates:

• Click on the "Estimates" or "Quotes" tab to create a new estimate.

Create a New Estimate:

• Look for the "New Transaction" or "New Estimate" button and click on it.

Fill in Customer Details:

• Select the customer or client from the drop-down menu or add a new customer if necessary.

• Ensure the customer's details are accurate and complete.

Enter Estimate Details:

• Input the estimate date (the date the estimate is created) and the expiration date if applicable.

Add Products/Services to the Estimate:

• In the "Product/Service" column, start typing the name of the item or service you're estimating for.

• Select the item or service from the drop-down list or add a new one if it's not in your list of products/services.

• Enter the estimated quantity, rate, and any applicable discounts or taxes.

Include Additional Notes (if needed):

• Add any additional information or notes relevant to the estimate in the provided sections.

Save the Estimate:

• Review all details for accuracy.

• Once reviewed, click "Save and close" or "Save and new" to save the estimate.

Send the Estimate (optional):

• If you're ready to send the estimate to the customer, click on "Save and send" to email the estimate directly from QuickBooks Online.

• Alternatively, save the estimate and send it later via email or print a hard copy to share with the customer.

Track the Estimate Status:

• Monitor the status of your estimates in the "Estimates" section to track whether they've been accepted, declined, or are still pending.

Notes:

• Customize estimate templates in the "Custom Form Styles" section within Account and Settings to match your business's branding and preferences.

• QuickBooks Online allows you to easily convert estimates into invoices once they are accepted by the customer.

• Regularly follow up on estimates to encourage decisions or address any inquiries from potential customers.

By following these steps, you can efficiently create estimates in QuickBooks Online, providing potential customers with detailed quotes for your products or services before finalizing a sale.

Sales receipts in QuickBooks Online are used to record sales for which payment is received immediately. Here's a step-by-step guide on how to create sales receipts:

Step-by-Step Guide to Creating Sales Receipts in QuickBooks Online:

Access the Sales Receipts Section:

• Log in to your QuickBooks Online account as an Admin or user with sales receipt permissions.

• From the left-side menu, select "Sales" or "Invoicing."

Navigate to Sales Receipts:

• Click on the "Sales Receipts" or "Customers" tab to create a new sales receipt.

Create a New Sales Receipt:

• Look for the "New Transaction" or "New Sales Receipt" button and click on it.

Fill in Customer Details:

• Select the customer or client from the drop-down menu or add a new customer if necessary.

• Ensure the customer's details are accurate and complete.

Enter Sales Receipt Details:

• Input the sales receipt date (the date of the sale) and a sales receipt number (if required).

Add Products/Services to the Sales Receipt:

• In the "Product/Service" column, start typing the name of the item or service sold.

• Choose the item or service from the drop-down list or add a new one if it's not in your list of products/services.

• Enter the quantity sold, rate, and any applicable discounts or taxes.

Include Additional Notes (if needed):

• Add any relevant notes or memos in the provided sections on the sales receipt.

Save the Sales Receipt:

• Review all details for accuracy.

• Once reviewed, click "Save and close" or "Save and new" to save the sales receipt.

Send the Sales Receipt (optional):

• If needed, email the sales receipt to the customer by selecting "Save and send" or save it to send later via email or print a hard copy.

Track Sales Receipt Status:

• Monitor the status of your sales receipts in the "Sales Receipts" section to keep track of completed transactions.

Notes:

• Customize sales receipt templates in the "Custom Form Styles" section within Account and Settings to match your business's branding and preferences.

• Sales receipts are used for transactions where payment is received immediately, such as retail sales or services rendered on-the-spot.

QuickBooks Online allows easy reporting and tracking of sales receipts for accurate financial records. By following these steps, you can efficiently create sales receipts in QuickBooks Online, accurately recording sales and immediate payments received from your customers.

HOW TO RECORD PURCHASE ORDERS ON QUICKBOOKS ONLINE

In QuickBooks Online, the creation of purchase orders allows businesses to request items or services from vendors. QuickBooks Online doesn't have a native feature specifically for purchase orders in all versions. Advanced plans or specific industries might offer this feature. For those versions that lack a dedicated Purchase Order feature, users often adapt the system to work for purchase orders by using customizations or other workarounds.

To simulate purchase orders in QuickBooks Online, you can create a workaround by utilizing the following steps:

Simulating Purchase Orders in QuickBooks Online:

Create a Custom Template or Use an Existing One:

• Utilize an existing template (like estimates or invoices) to represent your purchase orders. Customize it to include relevant information such as vendor details, item descriptions, quantities, costs, etc.

Use the Custom Template to Create Purchase Orders:

• Adapt the chosen template to serve as a purchase order by entering the necessary details for the items or services you wish to order from a vendor.

Save and Track Your Simulated Purchase Orders:

• Save these adapted documents as "Purchase Orders" or use specific naming conventions to distinguish them from other transactions.

• Track these documents manually or use designated fields to record order numbers, dates, vendor information, and itemized details.

Communicate Purchase Orders to Vendors:

• Share these adapted purchase orders with your vendors through email, print, or any preferred communication method to request the desired items or services.

Reference Purchase Orders in Transactions:

• Reference these simulated purchase orders in your transactions (e.g., bills, expenses, checks) to relate the received items or services to the original order.

Notes:

• This workaround might involve manual tracking and management of purchase orders outside of the standard QuickBooks Online purchase order functionality.

• Check if your version of QuickBooks Online provides the Purchase Order feature or consider upgrading to a plan that includes this functionality if essential for your business operations.

Remember, the availability of specific features in QuickBooks Online might vary based on the version or plan you're subscribed to. For comprehensive Purchase

Order functionality, you may need to explore QuickBooks Online Advanced or other specialized versions tailored for your industry. Always consult QuickBooks Online support or their official documentation for the most updated information regarding Purchase Orders in your specific version.

HOW TO RECONCILE BANK AND CREDIT CARD ACCOUNTS ON QUICKBOOKS ONLINE

Reconciling bank and credit card accounts in QuickBooks Online ensures that your financial records match your bank or credit card statements. Here's a step-by-step guide on how to reconcile bank and credit card accounts:

Reconciling Bank and Credit Card Accounts in QuickBooks Online:

Access the Reconciliation Section:

• Log in to your QuickBooks Online account as an Admin or user with reconciliation permissions.

• From the left-side menu, select "Accounting."

Choose Reconcile:

• Under the "Tools" section, select "Reconcile" next to the account you want to reconcile (bank or credit card).

Enter Reconciliation Details:

Fill in the required information:

• Account: Choose the bank or credit card account you're reconciling.

• Statement Date: Input the ending date of your bank or credit card statement.

• Ending Balance: Enter the ending balance shown on your bank or credit card statement.

• Beginning Balance (if applicable): If reconciling for the first time, enter the beginning balance as per your statement.

Review Transactions:

• QuickBooks Online will display a list of transactions from your bank or credit card account for the specified period.

• Match these transactions with your bank or credit card statement, ensuring they're accurate and present.

Mark Transactions as Cleared:

• Check off each transaction in QuickBooks Online that matches your bank or credit card statement.

• As you tick them off, QuickBooks Online will automatically calculate the "Difference" between your records and the statement.

Handle Discrepancies:

• If the "Difference" is zero, your account is reconciled. Click on "Finish Now" to complete the reconciliation.

• If there's a "Difference," investigate and correct any discrepancies or missing transactions.

Finish Reconciliation:

• Once reconciled (i.e., the "Difference" is zero), click "Finish Now" to complete the reconciliation process.

Review Reconciliation Reports:

• After reconciliation, review the reconciliation reports to confirm accuracy and keep records for your files.

Additional Notes:

• Perform reconciliations regularly to maintain accurate financial records.

• Reconcile bank and credit card accounts monthly to catch discrepancies early.

• Address any discrepancies promptly to ensure accurate financial reporting.

By following these steps, you can reconcile bank and credit card accounts in QuickBooks Online, ensuring your records align with your actual bank or credit card statements, thus maintaining accurate financial data for your business.

HOW TO USE QUICKBOOKS ONLINE TO CREATE PROFESSIONAL INVOICES

Creating professional invoices in QuickBooks Online is a straightforward process. Here's a step-by-step guide to help you generate professional invoices:

Steps to Create Professional Invoices:

1. Access Invoicing Section:

• Login: Sign in to your QuickBooks Online account.

• Navigation: From the dashboard, navigate to the "+ New" button or the left-hand menu. Click on "Invoice" under the "Customers" or "Sales" section.

2. Enter Invoice Details:

• Customer Information: Select the customer you're invoicing or add a new customer if necessary. Ensure accurate contact information.

• Invoice Date and Number: Enter the date of the invoice and, if needed, customize the invoice number.

3. Add Products/Services:

• Itemize Line Items: Add products or services by selecting them from your pre-defined items list or create new items on-the-fly.

• Description and Quantity: Enter a description of each item/service, quantity, rate, and any applicable tax or discount.

4. Customize Invoice:

• Customization Options: Customize the invoice by adding your business logo, changing fonts, colors, or layout. Use the "Customize" button to access these options.

• Additional Details: Include payment terms, a personalized message, or any necessary notes to the customer.

5. Preview and Save:

• Review Invoice: Double-check all details, ensuring accuracy and professionalism.

• Save or Send: Save the invoice as a draft, or if ready, click "Save and Send" to email the invoice directly to your customer. You can also print or download it as a PDF.

Additional Tips:

• Recurring Invoices: Set up recurring invoices for regular billing cycles, saving time for repetitive invoicing.

• Payment Links: QuickBooks Online allows you to add payment links on invoices, making it easier for customers to pay online.

• Customer Statements: Generate customer statements summarizing all outstanding invoices for improved clarity.

Notes:

• Ensure your QuickBooks Online account is set up with accurate products/services and customer information for efficient invoicing.

• Regularly update payment terms and invoice templates to align with your business requirements or any changes in policies.

Following these steps will enable you to create professional-looking invoices using QuickBooks Online, allowing you to efficiently bill your customers while maintaining a polished image for your business.

CHAPTER FOUR

HOW TO GENERATE VARIOUS FINANCIAL REPORTS ON QUICKBOOKS ONLINE

Creating financial reports in QuickBooks Online provides valuable insights into your business's financial health and performance. Here's a step-by-step guide on how to generate various financial reports:

Step-by-Step Guide to Generating Financial Reports in QuickBooks Online:

Access Reports Section:

• Log in to your QuickBooks Online account as an Admin or user with report access.

• From the left-side menu, select "Reports."

Choose a Report Category:

• QuickBooks Online provides various report categories like "Standard," "Business Overview," "Sales," "Expenses," "Profit and Loss," "Balance Sheet," etc.

• Click on the category that corresponds to the type of report you want to generate.

Select a Specific Report:

Within the chosen category, select the specific report you want to generate. For example:

• Profit and Loss Statement: Analyzes your income and expenses over a specific period.

• Balance Sheet: Provides a snapshot of your company's financial position at a given point in time.

• Cash Flow Statement: Displays your cash flow over a period, detailing cash inflows and outflows.

• Aging Reports: Shows the age of outstanding customer invoices or vendor bills.

• Sales by Customer Detail: Displays sales breakdown per customer.

• Expense Reports: Provides a breakdown of your expenses by category.

Set Report Parameters:

• Once you select a specific report, set the parameters such as date range, accounting method, customization options, and filters based on your requirements.

Run the Report:

• Click on "Run Report" or similar options to generate the selected report based on the specified parameters.

Customize Report (if needed):

• Utilize customization options within the report to adjust columns, add or remove data fields, change date ranges, apply filters, or modify settings to tailor the report to your preferences.

Save or Export the Report (optional):

• If required, save the report by clicking on "Save Customization" for future use.

• Export the report in various formats like PDF or Excel by selecting the export option.

Review and Analyze the Report:

• Once the report is generated, review the data presented and analyze it to gain insights into your business's financial performance.

Repeat for Other Reports (if necessary):

• Repeat the process to generate additional reports or explore different categories to get a comprehensive view of your business finances.

Additional Notes:

• Familiarize yourself with various report categories and their purposes to choose the most relevant reports for your analysis.

• Experiment with customization options to tailor reports to your specific requirements for better insights.

• Save frequently used reports or customization settings for quick access in the future.

By following these steps, you can efficiently generate various financial reports in QuickBooks Online, providing you with valuable insights into different aspects of your business's financial health and performance.

HOW TO CUSTOMIZE REPORTS ON QUICKBOOKS ONLINE

Customizing reports in QuickBooks Online allows you to tailor the data, layout, and appearance of reports to better suit your business needs. Here's a detailed step-by-step guide on how to customize reports:

Step-by-Step Guide to Customizing Reports in QuickBooks Online:

Access Reports Section:

• Log in to your QuickBooks Online account as an Admin or user with report access.

• From the left-side menu, select "Reports."

Choose a Report:

• Select the report you want to customize from the various categories available (e.g., Profit and Loss, Balance Sheet, Sales, Expenses, etc.).

Run the Report:

• Click on the report to open it or choose "Run Report" to generate the default report.

Customize Report Settings:

• Look for the "Customize" or "Customize Report" button at the top-right corner of the report window and click on it.

Set Report Date Range:

• Adjust the date range to view data for a specific period. Choose from preset ranges or set a custom date range.

Customization Options:

• Rows/Columns: Add, remove, or rearrange columns to display the data you want to analyze.

• Filters: Apply filters to include or exclude specific data based on criteria such as accounts, customers, date ranges, etc.

• Headers/Footers: Customize headers or footers by adding or removing company information, titles, or additional notes.

• Fonts and Styles: Modify fonts, font sizes, and styles to improve readability or match your branding.

• Display Columns by Months/Quarters/Years: Adjust the display of data columns based on time intervals for better analysis.

• Subtotal Rows: Include or exclude subtotal rows to summarize data within the report.

• Group by: Group data by specific criteria like date, customer, product, etc.

Preview Changes:

• As you make adjustments, preview the report to see how the changes affect the data presentation.

Save Customization (if needed):

• If you plan to use this customized report in the future, save the customization by clicking on "Save Customization" and provide a name for easy access later.

Run the Customized Report:

• Once satisfied with the customization, click on "Run Report" to generate the customized report with your specified settings.

Export or Print (if needed):

• Export the report to Excel, PDF, or print it for further analysis or sharing.

Notes:

• Experiment with different customization options to see which settings provide the most useful information.

• Save frequently used customized reports for quicker access in the future.

• QuickBooks Online remembers the most recent customization settings for each report, making it easier to access your preferred view.

By following these steps, you can effectively customize reports in QuickBooks Online, tailoring the data presentation to your specific business requirements for better analysis and decision-making.

UNDERSTANDING AND INTERPRETING FINANCIAL DATA

Understanding and interpreting financial data is crucial for assessing a business's performance, making informed decisions, and planning for the future. Here's a guide on how to approach and interpret financial data effectively:

Know the Basics:

Financial Statements:

Familiarize yourself with fundamental financial statements:

• Balance Sheet: Shows assets, liabilities, and equity at a specific point in time.

• Income Statement (Profit and Loss): Displays revenues, expenses, and profits over a period.

• Cash Flow Statement: Illustrates cash inflows and outflows during a specified period.

Financial Ratios:

• Learn key financial ratios (e.g., liquidity, profitability, solvency) used to analyze a company's financial health.

Review Financial Statements:

• Balance Sheet Analysis: Assess the company's liquidity (ability to meet short-term obligations) and solvency (long-term financial health).

• Income Statement Analysis: Evaluate revenue trends, cost structure, and overall profitability.

• Cash Flow Analysis: Analyze cash from operating, investing, and financing activities to understand cash position and operational efficiency.

Perform Ratio Analysis:

• Liquidity Ratios: Assess the company's ability to meet short-term obligations (e.g., Current Ratio, Quick Ratio).

• Profitability Ratios: Measure the company's ability to generate profits relative to sales, assets, or equity (e.g., Gross Margin, Net Profit Margin).

• Solvency Ratios: Evaluate the company's ability to meet long-term obligations (e.g., Debt-to-Equity Ratio, Interest Coverage Ratio).

Identify Trends and Patterns:

• Comparative Analysis: Compare financial data across different periods to identify trends, growth, or declines.

• Benchmarking: Compare your company's financial ratios and performance against industry standards or competitors.

Understand Non-Financial Metrics:

• Operational Metrics: Consider non-financial indicators like customer satisfaction, employee turnover, market share, etc., which impact financial performance.

Ask Questions and Seek Insights:

• Critical Thinking: Question anomalies or unexpected trends in the data to understand underlying causes.

• Seek Insights: Discuss financial reports with accountants, financial advisors, or industry experts for valuable perspectives.

Use Data for Decision-Making:

- Strategic Planning: Utilize financial data to make informed decisions, set goals, and formulate strategic plans.

- Course Correction: Adjust strategies based on the insights gained from analyzing financial data.

Continuous Learning and Improvement:

- Stay Updated: Keep learning about new financial metrics, market trends, and best practices in financial analysis to enhance your understanding.

Tools and Software:

- Financial Software: Leverage financial software like QuickBooks Online, Excel, or specialized analytics tools for easier data interpretation and analysis.

Effective Communication:

- Reporting and Presenting: Present financial data in a clear, concise, and visually appealing manner for better communication with stakeholders.

Understanding and interpreting financial data is an ongoing process that involves a mix of analytical skills, industry knowledge, and an understanding of the business environment. Regularly reviewing and analyzing financial information helps in making informed decisions and driving business growth.

HOW TO INTERPRET DATA ON QUICKBOOKS ONLINE

Interpreting data in QuickBooks Online involves analyzing the information presented in various reports to gain insights into your business's financial health and performance. Here's a step-by-step guide on how to interpret data in QuickBooks Online:

Step-by-Step Guide to Interpreting Data in QuickBooks Online:

Access Reports Section:

• Log in to your QuickBooks Online account as an Admin or user with report access.

• From the left-side menu, select "Reports."

Choose a Relevant Report:

• Select a report that aligns with the aspect of your business you want to analyze (e.g., Profit and Loss, Balance Sheet, Cash Flow, Sales by Customer, Expense Reports).

Run the Report:

• Click on the desired report or "Run Report" to generate the default view of the selected report.

Review Key Metrics:

Identify and focus on key metrics presented in the report:

• Profit and Loss (Income Statement): Revenue, expenses, gross profit, net income.

• Balance Sheet: Assets, liabilities, equity.

• Cash Flow Statement: Operating, investing, and financing activities.

• Sales Reports: Revenue by customer, product, or service.

• Expense Reports: Breakdown of expenses by category.

Analyze Trends and Patterns:

Look for trends or patterns over time:

• Are revenues increasing or declining?

• Are certain expenses consistently high?

• Are there seasonal fluctuations in sales or expenses?

Compare Periods:

Compare current data with previous periods (month-to-month, quarter-to-quarter, year-over-year):

• Identify growth or decline in revenue, expenses, and profits.

• Assess changes in financial ratios or key performance indicators.

Spot Anomalies or Discrepancies:

Identify outliers or unexpected data points:

• Investigate irregular spikes or drops in income or expenses.

• Review discrepancies between actual figures and budgeted amounts.

Use Filters and Customization:

Utilize report customization options to focus on specific data subsets:

• Apply filters by date range, accounts, customers, or other relevant criteria.

• Customize columns or display options to better analyze data.

Apply Financial Ratios and Metrics:

Calculate and interpret key financial ratios (liquidity, profitability, solvency):

• Assess liquidity using ratios like Current Ratio or Quick Ratio.

• Evaluate profitability using ratios like Gross Margin or Net Profit Margin.

• Measure solvency using ratios like Debt-to-Equity Ratio or Interest Coverage Ratio.

Draw Insights and Make Decisions:

Use the interpreted data to derive insights and make informed decisions:

• Identify areas for cost reduction or revenue enhancement.

• Make strategic decisions based on financial insights.

• Adjust business strategies or budgets as needed.

Notes:

• Ensure you understand the context and significance of each report and its components within your business operations.

• Regularly review and analyze financial data to track performance and make informed decisions for business improvement.

Interpreting data in QuickBooks Online involves using the presented information to understand your business's financial position, performance, and trends. Regular analysis of these reports is crucial for informed decision-making and strategic planning.

HOW TO SETUP AND PROCESS PAYROLL ON QUICKBOOKS ONLINE

Setting up and processing payroll in QuickBooks Online involves several steps to ensure accurate payroll management for your business. Below is a step-by-step guide on how to set up and process payroll:

Step 1: Access Payroll Setup

Subscription Check:

• Ensure your QuickBooks Online subscription includes the payroll feature.

Access Payroll Setup:

• Log in to your QuickBooks Online account.

• From the left-side menu, go to "Employees" or "Payroll."

Set Up Payroll:

• If you haven't set up payroll, QuickBooks Online will guide you through the setup process.

• Click on "Set up payroll" or similar options to begin.

Follow On-Screen Instructions:

• QuickBooks will ask for information such as company details, tax information, employee details, pay schedules, etc.

• Provide accurate and complete information as requested during the setup process.

Connect Bank Account (for Direct Deposit, if applicable):

• Set up a direct deposit for paying employees, if desired, by linking your company's bank account.

Review and Confirm Setup:

• Once all necessary information is entered, review the setup details carefully.

• Confirm the accuracy of the information provided before finalizing the payroll setup.

Step 2: Run Payroll

Enter Employee Hours/Details:

• Input employee work hours, salaries, bonuses, deductions, or any other applicable details.

• Ensure accurate employee data for each payroll period.

Preview Payroll:

• Review the payroll details before processing to confirm accuracy.

• Check for errors or discrepancies in employee paychecks.

Process Payroll:

• Click on "Run Payroll" or similar options to process the payroll for the specified period.

Review Summary:

• After processing, review the payroll summary to ensure all calculations are accurate.

• Verify deductions, taxes, and net pay for each employee.

Approve and Confirm Payroll:

• Once satisfied with the payroll details, approve and confirm the payroll run.

Pay Employees:

• Pay employees either via direct deposit (if set up) or generate paychecks.

File and Remit Payroll Taxes:

• QuickBooks Online can help calculate payroll taxes. File and remit taxes as per legal requirements and deadlines.

Generate Pay Stubs:

• Provide employees with pay stubs displaying detailed payment information.

Record Payroll Transactions:

• Ensure payroll transactions are recorded accurately in your accounting records.

Notes:

• Regularly update employee information and tax rates to ensure accurate payroll calculations.

• Stay informed about payroll tax laws and compliance requirements to avoid penalties.

By following these steps, you can set up and process payroll efficiently in QuickBooks Online, ensuring accurate and timely payment to your employees while maintaining compliance with payroll tax regulations.

HOW TO TRACK INVENTORY ON QUICKBOOKS ONLINE

Tracking inventory in QuickBooks Online involves specific settings and processes to monitor and manage your stock levels accurately. Here's a step-by-step guide on how to track inventory:

Step 1: Enable Inventory Tracking

Access Company Settings:

• Log in to your QuickBooks Online account as an Admin or user with access to company settings.

Navigate to Account and Settings:

• Click on the Gear icon ⚙ at the top right and select "Account and Settings."

Choose Sales Tab:

• From the left-side menu, select "Sales."

Edit Sales Settings:

• Under "Sales form content," click on "Edit" next to "Products and services."

Check Inventory Tracking:

• Ensure the checkbox for "Track quantity and price/rate" is checked to enable inventory tracking.

• Save the changes.

Step 2: Set Up Inventory Items

Add Inventory Items:

• Go to the "Sales" or "Products and Services" menu.

• Click on "New" to add a new product or service.

• Select "Inventory" as the type and provide details like name, SKU, description, sales price, cost, and quantity on hand.

• Save the item.

Set Reorder Points (Optional):

• If needed, specify reorder points for items to know when to restock.

• Edit the inventory item and set a reorder point in the "Reorder point" field.

Step 3: Record Inventory Purchases and Sales

Purchase of Inventory:

• Go to the "+ New" button and select "Expense" or "Check."

• Enter the supplier, date, account details, and select the inventory item purchased.

• Input the quantity purchased and the cost.

• Save the transaction.

Sale of Inventory:

• Create a sales transaction (like an invoice or sales receipt).

• Add the customer details, date, and select the inventory item sold.

• Specify the quantity sold and the sales price.

• Save the transaction.

Adjust Inventory:

In case of adjustments (e.g., damaged goods, inventory count discrepancies):

• Go to the "+ New" button and select "Inventory Quantity Adjustment."

• Choose the adjustment date, inventory item, and input the quantity and value adjustments.

• Save the adjustment.

Step 4: Review Inventory Reports

Run Inventory Reports:

• Go to the "Reports" section and select "All Reports."

• Under "Sales and Customers," choose "Inventory Valuation Summary" or "Inventory Valuation Detail."

• Review these reports to see the current inventory levels, costs, and valuations.

Periodic Reconciliation:

• Perform periodic physical inventory counts to reconcile with QuickBooks Online records and adjust any discrepancies.

Notes:

• Regularly update inventory records for accurate stock levels and financial reporting.

• Consider integrating third-party apps for more advanced inventory management features if needed.

By following these steps, you can effectively set up and manage inventory tracking in QuickBooks Online, ensuring accurate records of your stock levels and transactions.

HOW TO MANAGE STOCK LEVELS ON QUICKBOOKS ONLINE

QuickBooks Online doesn't have a built-in inventory tracking feature in all versions. However, if your QuickBooks Online version supports inventory tracking, you can manage stock levels using the following steps:

Step 1: Enable Inventory Tracking

Access Company Settings:

• Log in to your QuickBooks Online account as an Admin or user with access to company settings.

Navigate to Account and Settings:

• Click on the Gear icon ⚙ at the top right and select "Account and Settings."

Choose Sales Tab:

• From the left-side menu, select "Sales."

Edit Sales Settings:

• Under "Sales form content," click on "Edit" next to "Products and services."

Check Inventory Tracking:

• Ensure the checkbox for "Track quantity and price/rate" is checked to enable inventory tracking.

• Save the changes.

Step 2: Add and Manage Inventory Items

Add Inventory Items:

• Go to the "Sales" or "Products and Services" menu.

• Click on "New" to add a new product or service.

- Select "Inventory" as the type and provide details like name, SKU, description, sales price, cost, and quantity on hand.

- Save the item.

Track Stock Levels:

- As you buy or sell inventory items, QuickBooks Online automatically adjusts stock levels based on transactions.

Inventory Adjustment (if needed):

To manually adjust inventory levels (e.g., for damaged goods or discrepancies):

- Go to the "+ New" button and select "Inventory Quantity Adjustment."

- Choose the adjustment date, inventory item, and input the quantity and value adjustments.

- Save the adjustment.

Step 3: Monitor Inventory Reports

Run Inventory Reports:

- Go to the "Reports" section and select "All Reports."

- Under "Sales and Customers," choose "Inventory Valuation Summary" or "Inventory Valuation Detail."

- Review these reports to see the current inventory levels, costs, and valuations.

Reconcile Physical Inventory:

- Periodically perform physical inventory counts to reconcile with QuickBooks Online records and adjust any discrepancies.

Notes:

- QuickBooks Online's inventory tracking feature availability varies by plan. Check if your subscription includes this functionality.

- For more advanced inventory management features, consider third-party integrations compatible with QuickBooks Online.

Always consult the latest QuickBooks Online support or documentation for the most up-to-date information and guidance on managing stock levels based on the features available in your specific version.

CHAPTER FIVE

INTEGRATION ON QUICKBOOKS ONLINE

Integrating other applications or services with QuickBooks Online can streamline your business processes by automating data transfers and improving efficiency. Here's a general guide on how to integrate third-party apps with QuickBooks Online:

Integrating Third-Party Apps with QuickBooks Online:

Step 1: Identify Compatible Apps

Research Compatible Apps:

• Explore the QuickBooks App Store or reputable software directories to find apps that integrate with QuickBooks Online.

• Look for applications that offer the functionalities or features you require.

Step 2: Choose and Install the App

Select the App:

• Choose the app that best fits your business needs and integrates seamlessly with QuickBooks Online.

Install the App:

• Access the QuickBooks App Store or the app's website to initiate the installation process.

• Follow the provided instructions to install the app and connect it to your QuickBooks Online account.

Step 3: Connect and Configure Integration

Authorize Access:

• When prompted, authorize the app to access your QuickBooks Online data.

Set Up Configuration:

• Follow the app's configuration steps to set up the integration.

• Configure settings, permissions, and preferences according to your business requirements.

Step 4: Test and Review Integration

Test Integration:

• After setup, perform test transactions or data transfers between the integrated app and QuickBooks Online.

• Verify that data is transferred accurately and in the desired format.

Review Functionality:

• Ensure that the integrated app functions as expected and meets your business needs.

• Check if data synchronization, automation, and reporting work efficiently.

Step 5: Monitor and Maintain Integration

Regularly Check Data Flow:

• Periodically review data synchronization between QuickBooks Online and the integrated app.

• Monitor for any discrepancies or errors in the data transfer.

Update and Maintain:

• Keep the integrated app updated with the latest versions or patches provided by the app developer.

• Address any issues promptly by contacting the app's support team or consulting their documentation.

Additional Notes:

• Integration Types: Integration methods may vary. Some apps might offer direct integrations through QuickBooks Online's API, while others might require configuration via third-party platforms like Zapier or Integromat.

• Documentation and Support: Follow the app's documentation or reach out to their support team for detailed instructions and troubleshooting guidance specific to that app.

Ensure to research thoroughly, read reviews, and confirm compatibility before integrating any third-party app with QuickBooks Online. Always adhere to best practices and security measures while granting access to your QuickBooks Online data to maintain data integrity and security.

HOW TO CONNECT WITH THIRD-PARTY APPS ON QUICKBOOKS ONLINE

Connecting third-party apps with QuickBooks Online involves using the Intuit Developer Platform or the QuickBooks App Store. Here's a general overview of the process:

Steps to Connect Third-Party Apps with QuickBooks Online:

Step 1: Explore the QuickBooks App Store or Intuit Developer Platform

QuickBooks App Store:

• Access the QuickBooks App Store (apps.intuit.com) or search for it within your QuickBooks Online account.

• Browse through the available apps categorized by function or industry.

Intuit Developer Platform:

• Go to the Intuit Developer website (developer.intuit.com).

• Explore the available developer resources, documentation, and tools.

Step 2: Select and Install the App

Choose an App:

• Select the third-party app that suits your business needs and integrates with QuickBooks Online.

Initiate Installation:

• Click on the chosen app to begin the installation process.

• Follow the prompts to authorize the app to access your QuickBooks Online data.

Step 3: Authorization and Integration Setup

Authorize Access:

• When prompted, grant permission for the app to access your QuickBooks Online company data.

- Follow the steps provided by the app to authorize access securely.

Configure Integration Settings:

- Set up configuration settings within the third-party app to specify how it interacts with QuickBooks Online.

- Configure permissions, data transfer frequency, mappings, etc., as required.

Step 4: Testing and Verification

Test the Integration:

- Perform test transactions or data transfers between the third-party app and QuickBooks Online.

- Verify that data is transferred accurately and in the desired format.

Review Functionality:

- Ensure that the integrated app functions as expected and fulfills your business requirements.

- Check for data synchronization, automation, and reporting functionalities.

Step 5: Monitor and Maintain Integration

Regular Monitoring:

• Periodically review data synchronization between QuickBooks Online and the integrated app.

• Monitor for any discrepancies or errors in the data transfer.

Keep Apps Updated:

• Update the third-party app with the latest versions or patches provided by the app developer.

• Address any issues or concerns by contacting the app's support team or referring to their documentation.

Notes:

• Intuit Developer Resources: The Intuit Developer Platform offers tools, APIs, and resources for developers to create and integrate apps with QuickBooks Online.

• Security Considerations: Ensure the third-party app provider adheres to security standards to safeguard your QuickBooks Online data.

• Support and Documentation: Refer to the app's documentation or support channels for detailed integration instructions and troubleshooting guidance specific to that app.

Always conduct thorough research, read reviews, and confirm compatibility before integrating any third-party app with QuickBooks Online.

API USAGE ON QUICKBOOKS ONLINE

Using the QuickBooks Online API allows developers to integrate and interact with QuickBooks Online data programmatically. The API enables access to various functionalities such as reading and writing data, managing transactions, customers, vendors, invoices, and more. Here's an overview of API usage on QuickBooks Online:

QuickBooks Online API Usage:

Step 1: Register Your App

Sign Up as a Developer:

• Register as a developer on the Intuit Developer Platform (developer.intuit.com).

• Create an account and log in to access developer tools and resources.

Create an App:

• Register a new app in the developer portal.

• Obtain credentials (Client ID and Client Secret) required for authentication.

Step 2: Authentication and Authorization

Obtain OAuth2 Access Token:

• Authenticate your app using OAuth2 authentication.

• Get authorization from the QuickBooks Online user to access their data.

Implement OAuth2 Flow:

• Use authorization flows (Authorization Code Flow, Implicit Grant Flow, etc.) to acquire an access token.

• Refresh tokens periodically to maintain access.

Step 3: Use API Endpoints

API Documentation:

• Refer to the QuickBooks Online API documentation for details on available endpoints, request/response formats, and parameters (developer.intuit.com/api).

Choose API Endpoints:

• Select the API endpoints based on the actions you want to perform (e.g., customers, invoices, transactions, reports).

Make API Requests:

• Use HTTP requests (GET, POST, PUT, DELETE) to interact with the API endpoints.

• Include the necessary headers, parameters, and payload in the requests.

Handle Responses:

• Process the responses received from the API calls.

- Parse the JSON or XML responses returned by the QuickBooks Online API.

Step 4: Development and Testing

Develop Integration:

- Develop the code in your preferred programming language using the QuickBooks Online API SDK or RESTful API.

Test API Calls:

- Test API calls using sandbox or test company data to ensure the functionality works as expected.

- Use the QuickBooks Online API sandbox environment for testing without affecting live data.

Step 5: Production Deployment

Deploy Integration:

- Once testing is successful, deploy your integration or application to the production environment.

• Implement error handling mechanisms to manage API errors gracefully.

• Use logging to track API usage and troubleshooting.

Notes:

• Rate Limits and Usage: Be mindful of QuickBooks Online API rate limits to avoid throttling or suspension of API access.

• Security Considerations: Securely store credentials and follow best practices to protect sensitive information.

• Versioning: Monitor and adapt to changes in the QuickBooks Online API versions to maintain compatibility.

Ensure compliance with Intuit's terms of service and API usage policies while developing applications or integrations with QuickBooks Online. Always refer to the latest documentation and guidelines provided by Intuit for accurate and updated information on API usage.

ADVANCED SETTINGS ON QUICKBOOKS ONLINE

QuickBooks Online offers various advanced settings and features that allow users to customize their accounting processes, automate tasks, and access more advanced functionalities. Here are some advanced settings and features available in QuickBooks Online:

1. Custom Fields and Customization:

• Custom Fields: Customize data fields to track specific information within transactions, customers, vendors, or items.

• Custom Form Styles: Create and customize sales forms (invoices, estimates) with advanced formatting, logos, and styles.

2. Automation and Workflows:

• Automated Workflows: Set up rules to automate repetitive tasks like categorizing transactions, sending reminders, or triggering actions based on specified conditions.

• Bank Rules: Create and manage bank rules to automatically categorize and process transactions.

3. Advanced Reporting:

• Custom Reports: Design and generate customized reports tailored to your business needs by selecting specific data fields, filters, and groupings.

• Report Groups: Organize and categorize reports into groups for easier access and management.

4. Inventory Management:

• Inventory Tracking: Track and manage inventory quantities, values, and adjustments (if enabled in your plan).

• Inventory Costing Methods: Choose between FIFO (First In, First Out) or Average Cost methods for valuing inventory.

5. Advanced Settings and Preferences:

• Chart of Accounts: Customize and organize the chart of accounts to reflect the specific financial structure of your business.

• Preferences: Access and adjust various preferences related to sales, expenses, payments, reports, and more to align with business requirements.

6. User Permissions and Roles:

• User Roles: Assign specific roles and permissions to users within QuickBooks Online to control access and functionality based on job roles.

• User Access Rights: Set restrictions on sensitive data and certain functionalities to maintain security.

7. Integration and Add-ons:

• Third-Party Integrations: Integrate QuickBooks Online with other applications and services for extended functionality or industry-specific features.

Accessing Advanced Settings:

• Gear Icon (Settings): Many advanced settings are accessible through the Gear icon ⚙ located in the top-right corner of the QuickBooks Online dashboard.

• Company Settings: Navigate to "Account and Settings" to access more detailed and advanced configurations for your company.

Notes:

• Advanced settings and features availability may vary depending on your QuickBooks Online subscription plan.

• Always refer to the most recent QuickBooks Online documentation or support resources for updated information on advanced settings and functionalities specific to your subscription level.

For the most accurate and current information on advanced settings and features in QuickBooks Online, checking the QuickBooks Online Help Center or contacting QuickBooks Online support directly is recommended.

CHAPTER SIX

ADDITIONAL FUNCTIONALITIES ON QUICKBOOKS ONLINE

QuickBooks Online offers a range of additional functionalities beyond its core accounting features. These additional functionalities provide users with enhanced capabilities to manage various aspects of their businesses efficiently. Here are some of the additional functionalities available in QuickBooks Online:

1. Multi-Currency Support:

• Multi-Currency Transactions: Perform transactions in different currencies and manage exchange rate fluctuations.

• Currency Gains and Losses: Track gains or losses due to currency fluctuations.

2. Project and Job Costing:

• Project Tracking: Allocate income, expenses, and time to specific projects or jobs.

• Job Profitability Analysis: Analyze the profitability of individual projects or jobs.

3. Time Tracking and Billable Hours:

• Time Tracking: Track employee work hours, assign billable hours to clients, and create timesheets.

• Invoicing for Time: Convert billable hours directly into invoices for clients.

4. Mileage Tracking:

• Mileage Deduction: Track and deduct business-related mileage for tax purposes.

• Reimbursement Calculation: Calculate and reimburse employees for business travel based on mileage.

5. Purchase Order Management:

• Purchase Order Creation: Create purchase orders to order goods or services from vendors.

• Order Tracking: Track purchase orders and link them to expenses or inventory.

6. Budgeting and Forecasting:

• Budget Creation: Set and track budgets for income, expenses, and accounts.

• Financial Forecasting: Estimate future financial performance based on current data.

7. Custom Reporting:

• Advanced Customization: Create customized reports using filters, groupings, and custom fields.

• Scheduled Reports: Set up and schedule reports to be generated and sent automatically.

8. Document Attachment and Storage:

• Attachment Functionality: Attach and store documents (receipts, contracts) directly within QuickBooks Online transactions.

• Document Management: Organize and access attached documents for easy reference.

9. Third-Party Integrations:

• App Integration: Integrate QuickBooks Online with various third-party applications to extend functionality (e-commerce, CRM, payment processors, etc.).

• Add-on Solutions: Access specialized add-on solutions for specific industries or business needs.

10. Accountant and Collaboration Features:

• Accountant Access: Collaborate with accountants or bookkeepers by providing access to financial data.

• Accountant Tools: Accountant-specific tools and functionalities for managing multiple clients.

Notes:

• Availability of additional functionalities may vary based on the specific subscription plan of QuickBooks Online.

• QuickBooks Online regularly updates and enhances its features, so it's essential to check their official resources for the latest functionalities available.

QuickBooks Online offers several time-saving shortcuts and best practices that can streamline your accounting tasks. Here are some of the most useful ones:

Time-Saving Shortcuts:

1. Keyboard Shortcuts:

• Ctrl + Alt + ?: Opens the shortcut help window displaying available keyboard shortcuts.

• Ctrl + Alt + N: Create a new transaction (like an invoice, expense, etc.).

2. Bank Feeds:

• Batch Actions: Use batch actions to categorize multiple transactions simultaneously.

• Rules: Set up rules to automatically categorize transactions based on specific criteria.

3. Customization and Templates:

• Custom Forms: Create custom invoice, estimate, or sales receipt templates to save time on data entry.

• Recurring Transactions: Set up recurring transactions for regular payments or invoices.

4. Search and Navigation:

• Search Bar: Use the search bar to quickly find transactions, customers, or vendors.

• Browser Tabs: Utilize multiple browser tabs to work on different transactions simultaneously.

5. Reports and Analysis:

• Custom Reports: Save frequently used custom reports for quick access.

• Export Reports: Export reports to Excel for further analysis or sharing.

Best Practices:

1. Regular Reconciliation:

• Frequent Reconciliation: Reconcile your bank and credit card accounts regularly to maintain accurate records.

2. Proper Chart of Accounts:

• Organized Chart of Accounts: Keep your chart of accounts clean and organized to simplify transaction categorization.

3. Automation and Integration:

• Utilize Apps: Integrate third-party apps that complement QuickBooks Online for enhanced functionality.

• Automate Recurring Tasks: Set up automated workflows for routine tasks.

4. Record-keeping:

• Document Attachments: Attach relevant documents (receipts, contracts) to transactions for easy reference.

• Consistent Data Entry: Ensure consistency in entering data to avoid errors and confusion.

5. Collaborate and Train:

• Collaborate with Professionals: Work closely with accountants or bookkeepers for better financial management.

• Training Resources: Use QuickBooks Online training resources to stay updated on features and best practices.

6. Stay Updated:

• Regular Updates: Keep your QuickBooks Online software up-to-date to access the latest features and improvements.

• Explore New Features: Stay informed about new features and updates released by QuickBooks Online.

7. Customer Support and Community:

• QuickBooks Support: Reach out to QuickBooks support for assistance with technical issues or queries.

• User Community: Join QuickBooks user communities or forums for tips, advice, and best practices.

By implementing these time-saving shortcuts and best practices, you can optimize your use of QuickBooks Online, improve efficiency, and maintain accurate financial records for your business. Always explore new features and functionalities to make the most out of the platform.

RECOMMENDED WORKFLOWS FOR DIFFERENT BUSINESS TYPES OR INDUSTRIES.

Different industries and business types often have unique workflows and requirements when it comes to managing finances and accounting. Here are recommended workflows tailored to specific industries or business types using QuickBooks Online:

1. Retail Businesses:

Sales and Inventory Management:

• Use QuickBooks Online's inventory tracking to manage stock levels, track sales, and reorder inventory when necessary.

• Set up categories for different product types and track sales by product category.

Customer Management:

• Utilize customer profiles to track customer purchases, preferences, and loyalty programs.

• Send customized invoices and receipts to customers.

Reporting:

• Generate reports on top-selling products, inventory levels, and sales performance by product category.

2. Service-Based Businesses:

Time Tracking and Billing:

• Use time tracking features to record billable hours for different projects or clients.

• Create invoices directly from billable time or expenses.

Client Management:

• Maintain detailed customer records to track services provided, agreements, and billing history.

• Set up recurring invoices for services rendered on a regular basis.

Expense Management:

• Categorize expenses related to services provided and allocate them to specific projects or clients.

3. Professional Services (Consultants, Agencies):

Project-Based Accounting:

• Set up projects or jobs within QuickBooks Online to track income, expenses, and profitability for each project.

• Allocate expenses to specific projects for accurate cost tracking.

Time and Expense Tracking:

• Use time tracking features to capture billable hours and allocate them to respective projects.

• Track reimbursable expenses incurred during client projects.

Reporting and Invoicing:

• Generate detailed reports per project or client, highlighting project profitability and expenses.

• Invoice clients based on detailed project breakdowns.

4. Real Estate:

Property Management:

• Use classes or locations to categorize income and expenses related to different properties.

• Track rental income, expenses, and property-related transactions separately.

Tenant Management:

• Maintain tenant records within QuickBooks Online and track rent payments, security deposits, and lease terms.

• Generate recurring invoices for rent payments.

Expense Tracking:

• Categorize property-related expenses (repairs, maintenance, utilities) and allocate them to respective properties.

5. E-commerce Businesses:

Sales and Fulfillment:

• Integrate e-commerce platforms with QuickBooks Online to sync sales data and streamline order processing.

• Track sales from different channels and platforms separately.

Inventory and Cost Management:

• Use QuickBooks Online's inventory features to manage stock levels and track cost of goods sold (COGS).

• Monitor inventory turnover and profitability by product.

Tax Management:

• Ensure accurate tax calculations and reporting for online sales by configuring tax settings.

Notes:

• Customizing workflows in QuickBooks Online is crucial to meet the specific needs of your business type or industry.

• QuickBooks Online's features and functionalities can be adapted to suit the requirements of various business types by utilizing custom fields, categories, and integrations.

• Regularly review and adjust workflows as your business evolves to optimize efficiency and accuracy.

Tailoring QuickBooks Online workflows to match the needs of your particular business type or industry is vital for efficient financial management. Always explore additional integrations, apps, or customizations that align with your specific business requirements.

In QuickBooks Online, users may encounter various issues while performing tasks or managing their accounts. Here are some common issues and their potential solutions:

1. Login and Access Issues:

Issue: Trouble logging into QuickBooks Online or accessing the account.

Solution:

• Check internet connectivity and ensure the correct login credentials are used.

• Clear browser cache and cookies or try using a different browser.

• Reset password if necessary through the "Forgot password" option.

• Contact QuickBooks Online support if login issues persist.

2. Bank Feeds and Transactions:

Issue: Bank transactions not updating or categorizing correctly.

Solution:

• Refresh the bank feed by selecting the "Update" button.

• Review and categorize transactions manually if automatic categorization is incorrect.

• Check for any bank feed errors and resolve them in the banking center.

• Reconnect the bank account if the connection is lost or experiencing issues.

3. Report Generation:

Issue: Unable to generate specific reports or encountering errors while generating reports.

Solution:

• Check for any filters applied that might limit the report data.

• Ensure the date range selected is accurate for the desired report.

• Try running the report in a different browser or device.

• If the issue persists, create a custom report with adjusted settings.

4. Slow Performance:

Issue: QuickBooks Online running slowly or experiencing performance issues.

Solution:

• Close unused browser tabs or applications running in the background.

• Clear browser cache and history regularly.

• Use a different browser or device to access QuickBooks Online.

• Check for system requirements and internet speed compatibility.

5. Invoice or Payment Problems:

Issue: Problems creating invoices, recording payments, or syncing payment data.

Solution:

• Verify invoice details and payment settings for accuracy.

• Re-enter payment information if there are issues with syncing payment data.

• Check for any outstanding payments or invoices that need reconciling.

6. Integration and Syncing Issues:

Issue: Difficulties with third-party app integration or data syncing.

Solution:

• Ensure that the integrated app is compatible with QuickBooks Online and properly configured.

• Review integration settings and permissions to resolve syncing problems.

• Reauthorize or reconnect the integrated app if the connection is lost or disrupted.

7. Tax Calculation Errors:

Issue: Incorrect tax calculations or problems with tax settings.

Solution:

• Review tax settings to ensure accurate tax rates and rules are applied.

• Double-check transactions for proper tax categorization.

• Consult with a tax professional or QuickBooks support for complex tax-related issues.

8. Error Messages and Notifications:

Issue: Receiving error messages or notifications within QuickBooks Online.

Solution:

• Note down the error message and search for the specific error code or description in QuickBooks Online support resources.

• Follow recommended troubleshooting steps provided for the specific error message.

• Contact QuickBooks Online support for assistance if the issue persists.

Notes:

• Always keep QuickBooks Online updated with the latest version and patches to avoid known issues.

• Backup important data regularly to prevent data loss in case of unexpected issues.

• When troubleshooting, document any steps taken and consult official QuickBooks Online resources or support for more complex issues.

For persistent or critical issues in QuickBooks Online, reaching out to QuickBooks Online support or consulting with a certified QuickBooks ProAdvisor might be necessary to resolve the problem effectively.

TIPS FOR OPTIMIZING QUICKBOOKS ONLINE USAGE

Optimizing your usage of QuickBooks Online can enhance efficiency and improve your accounting processes. Here are some tips to optimize QuickBooks Online usage:

1. Customize Settings for Your Business:

• Chart of Accounts: Tailor your chart of accounts to match your business structure and financial reporting needs.

• Preferences: Adjust settings in "Account and Settings" to align with your business preferences and workflows.

2. Regular Reconciliation:

• Bank and Credit Card Reconciliation: Reconcile accounts regularly to ensure accurate financial records and catch discrepancies early.

3. Utilize Automation:

• Bank Rules: Set up bank rules to automate categorization and streamline the transaction review process.

• Recurring Transactions: Use recurring transactions for invoices, bills, and other routine expenses to save time.

4. Embrace Integrations:

• Third-Party Apps: Integrate QuickBooks Online with compatible apps (e-commerce, CRM, payment processors) to extend functionality and automate data syncing.

• Add-ons: Explore and utilize add-on solutions for specialized tasks or industries.

5. Optimize Reporting:

• Customize Reports: Create custom reports to track specific metrics or analyze particular aspects of your business.

• Scheduled Reports: Schedule and automate report generation for regular review or sharing.

6. Streamline Customer and Vendor Management:

• Customer/Vendor Records: Keep detailed and up-to-date records for customers and vendors, including contact information and payment terms.

7. Enhance Security:

• User Permissions: Set appropriate user roles and permissions to control access and protect sensitive data.

• Regular Password Updates: Encourage users to update passwords regularly for enhanced security.

8. Stay Informed and Educated:

• Training Resources: Explore QuickBooks Online training materials, webinars, and tutorials to learn about new features and best practices.

• User Community: Join user communities or forums to exchange tips and advice with other QuickBooks users.

9. Document and Backup:

• Document Attachments: Attach supporting documents (receipts, contracts) to transactions for easy reference and record-keeping.

• Data Backup: Regularly back up your QuickBooks Online data to prevent loss in case of unforeseen circumstances.

10. Monitor and Review:

• Regular Review: Periodically review and audit your QuickBooks data for accuracy, errors, or inconsistencies.

• Financial Checkups: Conduct financial checkups to evaluate your business's financial health and identify areas for improvement.

11. Seek Professional Help When Needed:

• Consult with Experts: If faced with complex accounting issues or uncertain about certain functionalities, consider seeking advice from a QuickBooks ProAdvisor or an accountant.

By implementing these optimization tips, you can maximize the benefits of using QuickBooks Online, improve efficiency, and maintain accurate financial records for your business. Regularly reassess your workflows and adapt to new features or changes within QuickBooks Online to optimize your accounting processes further.

HOW TO REGULARLY BACK UP YOUR QUICKBOOKS ONLINE

QuickBooks Online automatically backs up your data and maintains a secure and reliable system. However, if you want to create additional backups for extra security or peace of mind, here are some recommended steps:

1. Export Data from QuickBooks Online:

• Reports and Lists: Use QuickBooks Online's reporting feature to generate reports for essential data such as balance sheets, profit and loss statements, customer lists, vendor lists, etc.

• Export Transactions: Utilize the export feature to download transaction data in formats like Excel or CSV files. Go to the specific transaction type (e.g., invoices, expenses) and select the option to export.

2. Use Third-Party Backup Services:

• Cloud Storage Services: Store exported QuickBooks Online data in secure cloud storage platforms like Google Drive, Dropbox, OneDrive, or similar services.

• Local Backup: Save data to your local computer or an external hard drive for an additional backup copy. Ensure proper security measures are in place for local storage.

3. Scheduled Backup:

• Manual Backup: Set up a routine to manually export and save essential QuickBooks Online data at regular intervals, ensuring you have updated copies.

• Automated Backup: Depending on the third-party service used, some cloud storage providers offer automated backup solutions. Explore options for scheduled backups within these services.

4. QuickBooks Online Data Export:

• Export Company Data: QuickBooks Online allows exporting company data as a backup. Navigate to "Settings" ⚙ > "Export Data" to create a backup file.

• Follow Instructions: Follow the instructions provided in QuickBooks Online to export and save your company data. This backup will contain information like lists, transactions, and attachments.

5. Consult QuickBooks Support:

• If you encounter difficulties or need specific guidance on backing up your QuickBooks Online data, consider reaching out to QuickBooks Online customer support. They can provide assistance and detailed instructions based on the latest features available in the software.

Notes:

• Regularly update your backup files to ensure they contain the most recent data.

• Maintain proper security measures for any backups, especially if stored locally or on personal devices.

• While QuickBooks Online has robust data security measures, creating additional backups is a good practice to mitigate risks associated with data loss or unexpected issues.

Keep in mind that backup practices and features within QuickBooks Online might have evolved since my last update. Always refer to the latest QuickBooks Online documentation or support resources for the most up-to-date and specific instructions on data backup procedures.

REAL WORLD EXAMPLES AND USE CASES THAT CAN HELP USERS SEE HOW TO APPLY QUICKBOOKS TO THEIR SPECIFIC BUSINESS NEEDS

QuickBooks Online offers diverse functionalities that can be adapted to various business types. Here are real-world examples and use cases demonstrating how different businesses can utilize QuickBooks Online:

1. Retail Business:

• Use Case: A retail store selling clothing and accessories.

• Inventory Management: Utilize QuickBooks Online's inventory tracking to manage stock levels, monitor sales trends, and automatically update inventory counts with each sale.

• Sales and Expenses Tracking: Record sales transactions, track revenue, and categorize expenses such as rent, utilities, and inventory purchases. Generate reports to analyze profitability by product category.

2. Service-Based Business:

• Use Case: A graphic design agency offering creative services.

• Time Tracking and Invoicing: Track billable hours using QuickBooks Online's time tracking feature.

Generate invoices directly from billable time, and record payments received from clients.

• Expense Tracking: Categorize expenses related to design software subscriptions, client meetings, or office supplies. Use reports to analyze project profitability and cost per client.

3. Construction Company:

• Use Case: A construction firm providing building and renovation services.

• Project Management: Set up projects within QuickBooks Online to track expenses, revenue, and profitability for each construction project. Allocate expenses to specific projects for accurate costing.

• Vendor Management: Manage subcontractors and material suppliers by recording bills and tracking payments. Use job costing reports to monitor project expenses against budgets.

4. E-commerce Business:

• Use Case: An online store selling electronic gadgets.

• Sales Tracking from Multiple Channels: Integrate the e-commerce platform with QuickBooks Online to automatically sync sales data. Categorize sales from different platforms and channels for detailed analysis.

• Inventory and Cost Management: Use QuickBooks Online's inventory features to manage stock levels, track cost of goods sold (COGS), and optimize inventory turnover.

5. Consulting Firm:

• Use Case: A consulting company offering business advisory services.

• Client Billing and Revenue Tracking: Generate invoices based on hourly rates or project fees. Track revenue streams from various consulting services.

• Financial Reporting: Use customized reports to analyze the profitability of different consulting projects, client retention rates, and revenue growth over time.

6. Food Service Business:

• Use Case: A restaurant or café offering dining and catering services.

• Sales and Expenses Tracking: Record daily sales, categorize expenses (e.g., food costs, utilities, payroll), and analyze profit margins using QuickBooks Online reports.

• Payroll and Employee Management: Process payroll for staff, track hours worked, manage tips, and calculate taxes using QuickBooks Online's payroll feature.

These use cases illustrate how different businesses can leverage QuickBooks Online to streamline accounting processes, manage finances efficiently, and gain valuable insights into their operations. QuickBooks Online's flexibility and features can be tailored to suit the specific needs and workflows of various industries and business types.

CONCLUSION

In conclusion, QuickBooks Online stands as a comprehensive and dynamic solution, revolutionizing the way businesses manage their financial tasks. Its user-friendly interface, robust features, and versatility cater to the diverse needs of businesses across various industries and sizes.

As a cloud-based accounting software, QuickBooks Online empowers users with accessibility, scalability, and efficiency. From streamlined invoicing, expense tracking, and insightful reporting to seamless integration with third-party apps, it simplifies complex financial processes, enabling businesses to focus on growth and strategy.

With continuous updates and innovations, QuickBooks Online adapts to evolving market trends and user demands, providing a platform that evolves alongside businesses. Moreover, its commitment to security, compliance, and customer support ensures a reliable and trusted tool for managing finances.

Whether it's a small startup, a growing enterprise, or an established firm, QuickBooks Online remains a vital ally in driving financial success. Its array of features, customization options, and optimization potential make it a cornerstone in the realm of accounting software, empowering businesses to thrive in today's dynamic economic landscape.

www.ingramcontent.com/pod-product-compliance
Lightning Source LLC
Chambersburg PA
CBHW072158290526
45794CB00004B/1561